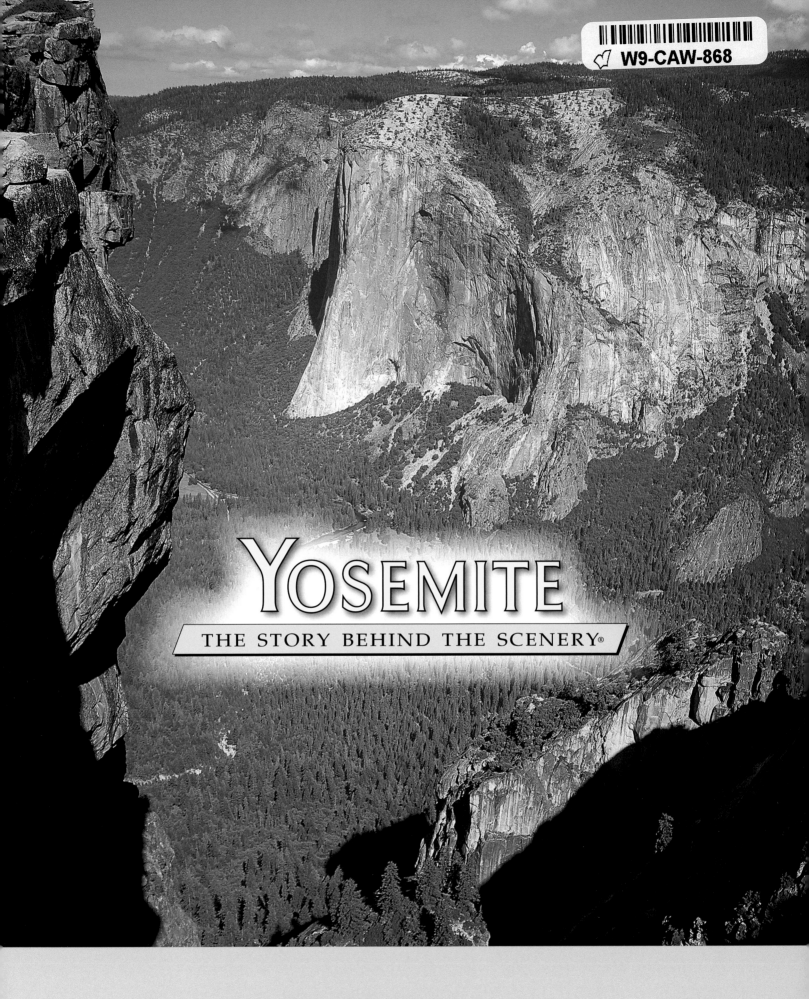

YOSEMITE

THE STORY BEHIND THE SCENERY®

by William R. Jones

WILLIAM R. JONES had an active career as a professional in interpretation and planning programs of the National Park Service. Bill's expert knowledge of Yosemite was gained through the 12 years he served there as a park naturalist.

Yosemite! Its cliffs and waterfalls are so high that the first explorers to see them could not begin to calculate their heights. Its landmark Half Dome is so distinctive in shape as to be unique in the world.

Its giant sequoia trees are so old that contemplation of their ages strains our human concept of time. And its High Sierra wilderness is so remote and vast that few have ever seen it all.

People from every corner of the United States—and the world—travel to this park in central California to gaze upon Yosemite's attractions and to marvel. And well they might, for Yosemite's features are truly awesome. Most come to see the unique Yosemite Valley, but the park has much more.

A prominent dimension to the Yosemite landscape is the infinite variety that the park encompasses. The range and diversity within this park is far too great to comprehend in a single visit, a time in which our thoughts are swept from the massiveness of El Capitan and the Sierran peaks to the delicacy of the tiny seedlings from which more giant sequoias will grow. Faced with such overwhelming evidence of nature's complexity, one cannot help but feel the wonder of the forces of creation.

It is this spirit of wonder that leads us to explore and investigate the marvelous detail that makes up the world of Yosemite.

A cluster of giant sequoias of the Mariposa Grove glow in winter sunbeams.

The Yosemite Story

Enhancing Yosemite's landscape is a dramatic change in topography. In a day's time, one's gaze can move two miles vertically from a warm canyon bottom up to the sight of Mount Lyell and its icy glaciers at 13,000-foot elevation. Four distinct seasons contribute to the park's breadth of interest, providing weather that ranges from the sunny days of summer—in which the sounds of birds and free-flowing streams blend in tuneful harmony, to the snowy, quiet days of winter—in which much of the park's high country is often locked in snows so deep that few venture to enjoy its pristine beauty.

With the astonishing variety of Yosemite, how could anyone fail to find something in the park that pleases?

If in autumn Bridalveil Fall is not at its boisterous springtime flow, it is still a remarkable sight, as its narrowed column sways to the side and separates into comet-shaped drops that are flung outward on the wind, so that the water seems no longer to fall but to hang suspended in a graceful, gravity-defying dance. If the solitude that one may crave is lacking on the floor of popular Yosemite Valley, isolation can be found in the expansive park wilderness. Then if the rock slopes of the high country begin to seem too stark and remote, one can return to the Sierran forests to enjoy the soothing companionship of tall conifers, elegant sequoia giants, and stately black oaks. Finally, there are stories of plants and animals, of early humans, and of explorers, settlers, artists, writers, and philosophers—all of whom found inspiration here and ultimately contributed to the park's place in the American—and world—mind and culture.

Yosemite Falls seems to drop from the sky, hurtling into a widening column that brushes into spray as it descends. The Upper Fall (1,430 feet) and the Lower Fall (320 feet) are separated horizontally by 1/3 mile of smaller drops and cascades (675 feet), making the combined Yosemite Falls (2,425 feet) among the highest in the world. It roars in late spring and drips in late fall.

View Yosemite Valley from above at Glacier Point. Look 3,200 feet down a nearly vertical cliff
*and see the meadows and seemingly tiny forest trees far below. Marvel at the famous Half Dome
and ponder its origin. Imagine glacial ice filling the deep valleys on each of Half Dome's sides almost to its
summit. Then extend that ice beyond to the Sierra crest on the horizon, and even cover Glacier Point,
where you stand, by hundreds of feet. North Dome, too, above Royal Arches at the left, was ice-covered.*

Far beyond
*Yosemite Valley
in the park's
eastern reaches
is a different
landscape than that of
cliffs, domes, and
waterfalls. Mount Gibbs
is a relict of the gentler
land into which Yosemite
and Hetch Hetchy
Valleys were carved.
This is the High Sierra,
Yosemite wilderness.*

*As profound as were mountain building
and stream and glacial processes
in forming Yosemite Valley,
these were but among the forces that
produced the masterpiece that is Yosemite.*

A Valley Is Carved

Many cliffs of Yosemite Valley are sheer. Near-vertical walls rise upward for more than half a mile. As we contemplate their massiveness and that of the majestic domes whose crowns are blazoned on the oft-blue sky overhead, questions as old as humankind crowd into our minds. How did the land get this way? What forces worked here to produce such a magnificent scene?

This spectacular landscape has been referred to as the "incomparable valley." But other valleys have similarities. Just north of Yosemite Valley, and still within the park, Hetch Hetchy Valley on the Tuolumne River is sometimes called the "Tuolumne Yosemite." Outside Yosemite National Park, but still in the same Sierra Nevada mountain range, are the magnificent valleys of the San Joaquin, Kern, and Kings Rivers. And one might compare also certain valleys of Alaska, Switzerland, and Scandinavia. These valleys have waterfalls and high cliffs and some have domes, but none surpasses Yosemite Valley's collection of these scenic elements.

That it is not a one-of-a-kind has not always been understood by geologists. Josiah Whitney apparently did not understand. In 1865 he explained the origin of Yosemite Valley and

JEFF GNASS

KATHLEEN NORRIS COOK

From Taft Point on the rim of Yosemite Valley,
*look down to the Merced River meandering past
El Capitan. El Capitan's "nose" rises steeply from
a base almost without talus (rock pile) to vertical
and then to an overhang in its upper third.*

Liberty Cap rises above Nevada Fall.
*The cap-shaped dome's flanks glisten, showing the
polishing effect of the glaciers that once slid past.*

Glacial erratic boulders lie where abandoned by the ice
stream that once moved down Tenaya Canyon on its way to Half
Dome, at right, and Yosemite Valley beyond. The ice scoured away soil to leave this area of
open bedrock as one of the most expansive anywhere.

JEFF GNASS

concluded that Half Dome had been "split asunder in the middle, the lost half having gone down in what may truly be said to have been `the wreck of matter and the crush of worlds,'" in which the bottom just "dropped out," producing the "exceptional creation" that is Yosemite Valley.

Whitney's explanation was accepted by most people at the time, for he was a noted expert, but among the doubters one was notable: John Muir engaged the origin argument head-on, stating, "the bottom never fell out of anything God made" and theorizing a glacial origin instead. In rebuttal Whitney dismissed such arguments as the daydreaming of a "mere sheepherder...an ignoramus."

A Shifting World

Today geologists accept the evidence that Muir carefully gathered to show the role of glaciers at Yosemite, but they are still studying other aspects of the origin of park features. Gradually, answers to old questions are being found, but in the process new questions continually present themselves.

One of these puzzles concerns the origin of marine fossils that are present in the rocks at the Sierra Nevada crest on the east side of the park, rocks that now lie as high as 13,000 feet above sea level yet are held solidly within strata that were clearly laid down in the ocean. Such rocks are also prevalent along the western boundary of the park, and there is also a thin, discontinuous band of them in the park's center. Were these rocks raised up from the sea? Did Yosemite and the entire Sierra Nevada range, some 400 miles long, rise as a great block of the Earth?

Plate tectonics holds that gigantic blocks of the Earth's sea floors are spreading apart from rift lines (into which new rock wells up from below). As the crustal plates move away from each other, they drift the continents with them. Massive global forces thus produce the Earth's broad relief features—ocean deeps and trenches, volcanic rises, flat plains and shallow seas, and continental mountains.

Some 500 million years ago is the earliest time that we know about anything in the Yosemite region, rocks and fossils of that era having left a record for our information. At that time a shallow sea stretched over what is now eastern California and western Nevada. Material that washed into this sea from adjacent land areas and erupted into it from volcanoes continued to be deposited over a vast period of time that lasted until about 100 million years ago.

Half Dome is seen edge-on, showing its tabular form. Its famous cliff face is at the left and its summit "beak" shows plainly. Left of the cliff face, cracks that had formed parallel to it allowed Ice Age glaciers to remove that part of Half Dome. Remnant stubs of cracked slabs from the "lost half" remain standing at a level about halfway up the cliff face, showing that actually only 10 to 15 percent has been lost. Winter snow mantles the dome and cloaks the High Sierra beyond.

FRED HIRSCHMANN

These conceptual landscape paintings recreate the changing geological scene of Yosemite Valley, spanning millions of years. Interpretations are based on studies of stream and landscape profiles, glacier traces, and comparisons with other glaciated regions.

1. The Merced River flows down the Sierra Nevada through a shallow valley. The resistant area that will become Half Dome (upper center) is being left by the eroding forces.

Overlapping the end of the above time period, from about 200 to 80 million years ago, massive slabs of rock from the Pacific Ocean sea-floor plate were moving eastward toward the North American continental plate. These sea-floor plate rocks (which were former oceanic sediments and volcanic deposits, and thus heavier) deflected under the lighter continental rocks, in *subduction*. Gradually the sea-floor plate rocks descended to such depths that, as temperature and pressure increased on them, they re-crystallized into harder metamorphic rocks. Volatile materials like water that they brought down with them lowered the melting point of the upper mantle and lower crust of the Earth, and portions of these melted.

GRANITES AND MORE GRANITES

The rocks below Yosemite turned to pasty fluid in three pulses at changing localities. The first occurrence caused granitic rocks to form around 200 million years ago in the eastern part of the park; some of these rocks are now exposed at Tioga Pass, the park's eastern road entrance. The second pulse occurred about 140 million years ago in the western part of the park, when most of the granitic rocks in the Sierra Nevada foothills and western Yosemite Valley were produced. The third pulse occurred about 85 million years ago in the park's center, forming the granitic rocks at the head of Yosemite Valley (such as Half Dome) and extending to Tuolumne Meadows.

Each melting pulse lasted 10 to 15 million years. Due to varying chemical components and differing cooling environments, each pulse also included sub-pulses that left rocks that can be identified and outlined on a map. Distinct kinds of granitic rocks were thereby produced—with characteristic minerals, textures, and colors. By noting the contact zones of these masses and by dating them with molecular clocks, the sequence of their formation has been chronicled.

Where a younger, still-fluid granitic mass came into contact with an older, solid one, the latter often would crack or have contained cracks from its own time of cooling or from earth movements. Pressure within the younger, still-fluid rock then injected material into the cracks in the older rock,

NATIONAL PARK SERVICE

4. The largest Ice Age glacier flows down the valley, smoothing projections and quarrying away lower slopes to shape a U. Half Dome is being carved into the form we know.

leaving tabular sheets when cooling was completed. If the older and younger rock contrasted much in color or texture, the basis was laid for the vein-like or mosaic patterns we see at the surface now that erosion has produced visible cross-sections of these contacts. In Yosemite Valley, these are especially noticeable on El Capitan's east wall.

These granitic rocks solidified perhaps five miles below the surface of the earth, probably underneath a mountainous region of volcanoes, lava flows, and ash deposits that typically forms above intruding granitic rocks. A similar landscape exists today at Yellowstone National Park, where steam geysers spout, heated by hot rock below. Erosion then slowly removed the ancestral volcanic mountains of the Sierra Nevada, and then much of the

2. Major Earth forces raise the Sierra Nevada higher and tilt it westward. The steepened Merced River runs faster and erodes more deeply. The future Half Dome continues to resist.

3. Continuing uplift causes the Merced River to sculpt a steep-walled canyon. Side streams are steepened less and so do not erode as deeply. Half Dome dominates.

5. The last of the glaciers flows through Yosemite Valley, covering only the lower valley walls. It dies at the valley's west end. Half Dome is revealed.

6. A lake forms in the shallow basin left by the last glacier. Streams bring silt and sand, and rocks fall in. Meadows and forests appear. Half Dome has formed.

underlying sedimentary and metamorphic rocks. Finally, about 70 million years ago, the erosion level reached the deep granitic rocks, which themselves then began to be eroded and carried by streams to be deposited westward. Because erosion can only work on higher ground, the Yosemite region must have been high at the start of this period of erosion or uplifted during it.

A NEW MOUNTAIN RANGE

At about 15 to 25 million years ago, the pattern of movement at the boundary between the ocean plate and the continental plate changed from sub-duction to *translation*. The ocean floor no longer dove under the continent. Instead, both plates now began moving westward, but with the ocean plate

The shifting ice shaped the valley and brought Half Dome to life.

Rays of a setting sun strike the westernmost valley walls. Leaning Tower overhangs its base, revealing the massive internal strength of this granitic monolith and providing an unusual challenge for those who climb its face. Dewey Point, a fine overlook into Yosemite Valley, is on the right.

SALVATORE VASAPOLLI

also still moving northward. Such a condition is not stable: the boundary between the plates is the highly active San Andreas fault on the west side of California, responsible for many earthquakes. Also at this time, the Sierra Nevada was continuing its rise, an uplift that goes on today, at a rate of about an inch per century at the range crest.

While the prior volcanic mountain range was being removed by erosion, the region was one of gentler relief with slower-moving streams. Deep soil formed. Just south of Yosemite the San Joaquin River drained across the Sierra Nevada from headwaters east of the present range crest. Remnants of this older regional surface persist. One is evident on the slopes of peaks near Tioga Pass on the eastern boundary of the park—such as gently sloping tablelands on North Peak and near Mount Dana. Another is the upland surface stretching back from the rim of Yosemite Valley.

Lavas flowed again, now on a new surface, mainly in the northern range, but as far south as

Yosemite's Tuolumne River drainage. Flows erupted into valleys and buried their stream channels.

About 5 to 10 million years ago, the Earth's crust stretched so much in an east-west direction that it cracked into a series of immense blocks between California and Colorado, known as the Basin and Range Province. The greatest of these blocks became the 400-mile-long Sierra Nevada. That block broke on the east, where the range now fronts Nevada; it tilted farther upward there but sank downward to the west under accumulating sediments in the Central Valley of California.

During this tilting, streams draining westward along the increasingly sloped block accelerated and eroded their valleys into canyons. They produced a new landscape of steeper slopes within the more undulating older contours. Within these older surfaces the Merced and Tuolumne Rivers carved V-shaped canyons typical of river valleys. Such canyons are still present today in the unglaciated downstream reaches of these rivers.

ICE ADVANCES

As the range was tilting upward on the east to its present height, the climate of the whole Earth began cooling, adding to the chilling effect of the higher altitudes being attained by the rising mountain block. This was about 2 million years ago. The Ice Age was beginning. About 1.3 million years ago, large glaciers began to form in the High Sierra. As these grew they began descending through stream canyons, exerting powerful force, polishing rocks that were hard and massive, quarrying rocks that were fissured, and carrying away loose soil formed in the prior warmer climatic period as well as the rock fragments now being crushed and pulverized by the ice. The moving ice cut away the lower walls of the valleys, straightening them, and transformed them from their V-shapes into U's, emphasizing with bolder strokes the land shaping that the streams had already begun.

The largest glacier (there may have been two or more this extensive) filled Yosemite Valley completely. It also extended down canyon ten miles to El Portal, 2,000 feet lower than Yosemite Valley. This glacier scoured the region for about 300,000 years until its demise about 1 million years ago.

The glacier or glaciers of this early period also gouged into the bedrock floor of Yosemite Valley, creating a trough below the present ground surface possibly as deep as 2,000 feet (postulated from seismic soundings and wells over 1,000 feet deep). This subsurface trough in the bedrock shallows at the valley's west end; there a shallowly buried bedrock lip remains. All the debris that eroded from the valley floor had to be lifted by the ice over this barrier.

Royal Arches shaped as massive lower portions of valley walls cracked and fell away, in exfoliation. North Dome, above, shows the rounding influence that exfoliation can exert in land shaping, although it was overridden by earlier glaciers.

JEFF GNASS

Horsetail Fall drops off El Capitan's shoulder, misting into its namesake form as an updraft comes up the cliff wall from Yosemite Valley below. Often this short-lived stream only wets the cliff where it hits, like a giant teardrop.

This was not impossible, because the slowly flowing ice was more than a mile deep in the upper valley and so had behind it the force needed. When this largest glacier finally died and melted away, it left much debris in the trough it had dug, as valley deposits.

Following the above ice episode, at least two more glaciers entered Yosemite Valley. These were much smaller. The first and larger peaked 130,000 years ago, and the last 20,000 years ago. These polished the lower valley walls but did not cut them back much. The last of these glaciers built moraine ridges at its terminus in the western end of the valley, arcing just west of El Capitan toward Bridalveil Fall, and acting as a natural dam when, about 15,000 years ago, this last glacier began melting, too. In the depression this last glacier had scoured in the valley deposits left by the earlier glaciers, a shallow lake formed (as others may have following earlier glaciations). This "Lake Yosemite" was almost seven miles long. Post-glacial rivers then filled the lake with silt and sand, and rock fell into the lake from canyon walls. Finally the lake—and the magnificent images that it undoubtedly reflected—vanished. In the area where it had lain, sedges and willows became established. Then, as other plants and trees gradually moved onto favorable valley sites, the broad meadow-and-forest floor we know today as Yosemite Valley began to develop.

HANGING VALLEYS

Unlike the larger and more powerful Merced River, which had a steeper course straighter westward down the tilted Sierran slope, side streams flowing in at angles to this course have not been able to cut as deeply into the rock. Thus, before the glaciers came, the side streams of Yosemite, Bridalveil, Ribbon, Sentinel, Illilouette, and other creeks dropped into the valley as cascades. When the earlier glacier or glaciers then passed down the main and tributary valleys, they, like the rivers before them, again eroded the main valley more deeply than the side valleys. Too, as the earlier of these main-valley glaciers widened the gorge, lower parts of the tributary valleys were cut back to leave the upper portions of these side valleys "hanging" even more and their streams falling in as almost-vertical cascades or waterfalls.

In the million years since, no glacier has reached high on the valley walls, and so cascading side streams in this long "recent" period have wetted their rock slopes with spray. This, coupled with repeated freezing and thawing, allowed most of these side streams to erode recesses in the bedrock.

In this canyon dubbed a giant stairway, Vernal Fall drops down the final riser. Spray it generates gives the name for the Mist Trail leading to the fall's top. Up canyon is another tread and riser in this stairway—Nevada Fall.

In the Valley

A raucous call from a Steller's jay will likely be your first animal experience in Yosemite Valley. You may see deer, and you might encounter a bear. Seeing ground and gray squirrels as well as chipmunks is almost assured. There is a good chance of also spying their coyote predator, and maybe even a bobcat, skunk, weasel, or raccoon.

Other bird species you may see include evening grosbeak of the ponderosa pine forests; cliff-dwelling white-throated swift; canyon wren, which may sing its descending scale of notes for you at cliff bottoms; dipper, bird of rushing streams; mountain quail with its topknot feather; and many more.

Reptiles include toads, frogs, and snakes, mostly non-venomous, but there are poisonous rattlesnakes.

White flowers of Pacific dogwood grace the valley's woods in springtime and the western azalea then livens the open meadows. Lavender lessingia blooms early and keeps going into autumn when meadow goldenrod joins in contrasting color.

A raccoon angler uses "fingery" paws to catch fish hiding under stream rocks. Mainly nocturnal, raccoons look like masked four-legged bandits and have a characteristic ringed tail.

FRANK S. BALTHIS

Snow plant emerges from forest duff when winter snow melts. It is a saprophyte, a plant that obtains its food from dead or decaying organic matter. It has no chlorophyll, the green color that most plants have. The scientific name—Sarcodes sanguinea—speaks of its bright blood-red color.

EDA ROGERS

Bridalveil Fall and Upper Yosemite Fall are different, as both still leap boldly into the valley. Bridalveil Fall may do so because the monolith of its brink is too durable for the stream to erode effectively. Upper Yosemite Fall makes its clear leap because it is spouting out of a "new" (less than 130,000 years old) channel instead of the steep gully it had followed for millions of years, just west of the present fall. One of the later glaciers coming down Yosemite Creek above Yosemite Valley appears to have diverted the stream to this new channel. Spray wetting the bases of both Upper Yosemite and Bridalveil Falls appears to have eroded their bases and further steepened them.

Streams now dropping into Yosemite Valley have thereby come to be some of the highest and steepest waterfalls in the world. Waterfalls on the main Merced River, however, such as Vernal and Nevada Falls, not having the hanging valley situation, drop over steps cut where fractures allowed the ice to erode more effectively.

Protecting its nest, this brown trout hovers over a pocket in stream gravel. Not native to Yosemite, this and other introduced trout species that compete with indigenous rainbow trout and other natural aquatic life are no longer being stocked in the park.

Forest-floor litter by the mouthful heads for this California ground squirrel's underground nest.

Already always on the alert, this fawn peeks over its mother doe. Many Yosemite deer migrate into the High Sierra for summer, and then in autumn back down to winter range. Mature males—bucks —grow and shed antlers yearly.

What is exfoliation? Exfoliation is the process in which rock shells or tabular layers are cast off as the rock expands. Exfoliation is usually the result of heat, freezing, or the absorption of moisture, but these localized effects can hardly account for the scale on which exfoliation occurs on Yosemite's massive domes and cliffs. For example, the exfoliation plates showing prominently on the Royal Arches rock formation are as thick as 200 feet, and some extend for hundreds of yards. At Yosemite exfoliation *by load relief* is a dominant land-shaping process.

Yosemite's rocks were once buried perhaps as much as five miles below the surface of the Earth. Once at the surface, these rocks expanded into the void, since they were no longer subjected to the pressure under which they were formed. Cracks slowly formed parallel to exposed surfaces, creating layers that broke away. Angularities were thereby subdued, and rounded forms developed. Because of the many occurrences of un-fissured rocks in Yosemite, such exfoliation is especially prominent. Had more fractures been present, other forms of erosion would have prevailed. (Rock types other than granitic rocks exfoliate, too. Consider the massive sandstones of the cliffs in Zion National Park and the similar rock formations at Glen Canyon National Recreation Area, both in Utah.)

None of Yosemite's domes is perfectly round. A few seem to have split, the result of the influence of joints (comparable to master cracks in a masonry

At a meadow border sun shines through a pine while low mist and high fog give mystery to the towering walls. Yosemite Valley shows a myriad of moods.

CRACKS ARE THE KEY

Are Yosemite's spectacular domes products of glaciers? True, the earlier glacier or glaciers over-rode some of the domes, such as those on the north side of the valley—North Dome, Basket Dome, and Mount Watkins. But never did a glacier completely cover domes to the south—Half Dome, Sentinel Dome, and Mount Starr King. The summit of Half Dome, for example, is estimated to be 3 to 10 million years old, shaped before the Ice Age. Even if these Yosemite examples do not convince that glaciers do not shape all domes, there is proof in the domes of Stone Mountain, in Georgia, and those of Rio de Janeiro, in Brazil, none of which ever knew the raspy touch of a glacier. It is *exfoliation*, not glaciation, that forms domes.

wall), another important element that has shaped Yosemite Valley. Joints may be tiny cracks or just planes along which pressure or friction has weakened rock crystals or their bonds, and along which fluids pass more readily. Joints provide avenues for more rapid erosion than can occur in solid rock. In The Fissures at Taft Point only local snowmelt or raindrops trickle into the cracks, yet because of master joints there the effect is deep, open gashes in the otherwise unjointed rock.

Effects of joints are further shown at Yosemite Falls where two long horizontal ledges have developed on joint planes. One joint-ledge is at the Upper Fall's base and the other is at the Lower Fall's top, controlling the location of these scenic elements. The Three Brothers, symmetrically angled

DIANNE DIETRICH LEIS

Originally a monolith of granite, obviously with a fracture plane, Half Dome is today the remnant of glacial action. The Valley's form allowed the sweep of glacial forces to "take away" its North Face's North side and leave the sheer wall on the Northwest side for us to see and photograph in all seasons.

rock summits on the north side of Yosemite Valley, are formed where parallel joint sets intersect, the most prominent set sloping about 45 degrees downward to the west. And of course there is Half Dome: its face is the remaining side of a block cracked by joints along which glaciers quarried away the lost "half" (actually much less than half). Too, the Half Dome face follows the same vertical, northeast-southwest trend that is the principal joint pattern in Yosemite. Tenaya Canyon and many canyons and streams located north of the Tuolumne River, as well as zigzagging portions of Yosemite Valley itself, also follow the regional trend along vertical joints both exposed and concealed.

Just as joints can control the topography, so can the *absence* of joints. El Capitan is the best example. Only discontinuous cracks flaw the bold faces of this monolith, which stands at the narrowest part of the valley, opposite the similarly-massive Cathedral Rocks. Both the opposing El Capitan and Cathedral Rocks formations are made up largely of the same strong granitic rock type (known as El Capitan Granite), from a wide band that apparently once crossed the valley here. Each of these formations is so little cracked that virtually no rock has fallen to pile at its base. Its sparseness of joints makes El Capitan a world-class climber's challenge, and the Cathedral Rocks has similar

Peregrine falcons nest in cavities or on ledges high on Yosemite's cliffs. "Fighter-jets" of the bird world, they prey on other birds, small mammals, insects, and fish.

RICHARD CUMMINS

TODAY—AND BEYOND

The aspect and appearance of the awesome Yosemite Valley is due to factors that are inherent in the locality: the internal character of its rocks—their chemistry, mineralogy, texture, and grain size—and the way they fractured or did not fracture in response to forces exerted upon them. Streams and glaciers could not erode the rocks that were too strong and left these as massive outcroppings that have exfoliated into sheer cliffs, some with waterfalls, and the rounded domes that we see today. Weaker rocks that once surrounded these features have succumbed to erosion; thus the formations that are left now stand out in solitary splendor.

Land shaping is a process that never ends. In the time since the Ice Age glaciers melted away, rockslides have fallen, waterfalls have eroded their bases to drop more steeply, and the last Lake Yosemite has been filled. The Merced River now meanders where that ancient lake once shimmered. Nature's work goes on. Just as Yosemite does not now appear as it once did, so will it be different in the future. We are seeing it at only one brief moment in time. Perhaps someday all this will be no more; or perhaps nature's agents will restore the glaciers and the valley lake, or somehow create a different landscape that is more beautiful still. We can only enjoy and cherish Yosemite as it is today, at the same time marveling at nature's ability to create and alter and create again. Wonder is the special province of humans, and there is no better place to renew this precious quality than at Yosemite, a gift of creation.

SUGGESTED READING

HILL, MARY. *Geology of the Sierra Nevada*. Berkeley: University of California, 1975.

HUBER, N. KING. *The Geologic Story of Yosemite National Park*. Yosemite, California: Yosemite Association, 1989.

JONES, WILLIAM R. *Domes, Cliffs, and Waterfalls: A Brief Geology of Yosemite Valley*. Yosemite, California: Yosemite Association, 1991.

MATTHES, FRANCOIS E. *The Incomparable Valley: A Geologic Interpretation of the Yosemite*. Berkeley: University of California, 1950.

climbs. Both, however, have overhanging slabs that will come down some day.

And so joints form differently in different types of rock, and in Yosemite Valley eight major types of granitic rocks—each with different characteristics—have been mapped. Each type has its own jointing "personality" that has influenced the scenery where that rock type occurs.

At the opposite, eastern, end of the valley from El Capitan and Cathedral Rocks, prominent Sentinel Dome standing above the valley rim is also composed of El Capitan Granite. There, too, stand the rest of Yosemite Valley's main domes: North Dome, Basket Dome, Mount Watkins, Half Dome, Mount Broderick, Liberty Cap, and the Starr King group. These are all composed of another, similarly strong, granitic rock called Half Dome Granodiorite. These two sparsely jointed rock types (named after their most prominent examples at El Capitan and Half Dome) constitute virtually all of the outstanding domes and cliffs present around Yosemite Valley.

Massive El Capitan appears as a ship's prow projecting into forests lining the tranquil Merced River.

Overleaf: Midsummer wildflowers bloom at treeline near Tioga Pass. Higher, slopes still hold snow. Photo by Kathleen Norris Cook.

The High Sierra–A Bold Land

GLENN VAN NIMWEGEN

Contrast marks Yosemite's High Sierra—rock, water, and sky come together in bold edges: deep-blue lakes lap against pale granite shores, rock spires thrust toward billowy thunderheads, and streams flash in the sun like slivers of crystal.

The High Sierra landscape looks like what it is—a land just created. Its sculptors—glaciers—are mainly gone now, and have been for some 15,000 years, but their trails shine on in this fresh and ex-hilarating atmosphere. Even the rocks gleam.

There is a stark rawness here that all of life seems to sense: Deer pause at meadow borders, trees assume bonsai forms in lines along joint cracks, and pikas call in squeaky tones from under jagged boulder piles.

***B**ands of pine pollen plaster* boulders at a High Sierra lake's edge, marking stands of water as levels dropped from spring highs. Alpine laurel brightens the scene now, but ice and snow dominate most of the year.

KATHLEEN NORRIS COOK

ICE IS THE SCULPTOR

High on the shaded ridges of Yosemite's highest point—13,114-foot Mount Lyell—the glacier trails are the freshest of all. In fact, living glaciers are there now. Today's glaciers are not remnants of the past; they are new, having formed and perhaps reformed within the last two or three thousand years, a period of time that approximates modern human history. While looking at the reality of these living glaciers, the question of whether the Ice Age is over seems out of place.

Above the Lyell Glacier during the long winters, howling winds blow falling snow over the peak into the great canyon heads all around. There the once-light flakes pile so deeply that, under their weight, their bottom layers turn to ice and begin to move away from the overburdening pressure, flowing down the slopes due to gravity. Thus glaciers are born.

Today the crevasse at the head of Lyell Glacier, its *bergschrund*, is again near the place where one was during the Ice Age. Again, water from melting snow flows into the bergschrund, entering the cracks in the rocks below, freezing there in the cold of the shadows and widening the cracks. As the resultant expansion splits and shears the rock, blocks of it lodge in the adjacent ice mass and begin the journey downslope. Now, however, they do not journey very far: the boulders come up

Yosemite's High Sierra is a bold land of granitic expanses, domes, ridges, and peaks— softened by pockets of forest and meadow, shimmering lakes and glinting cascades. It is a young land where streams seem to wander about before selecting their paths. It is a land "just" (this was 15,000 years ago) released from the glaciers. On the central ridge, the high point is Fairview Dome; it was buried by the ice. At the left of the scene, angular peaks stand high on the horizon beyond; they were free of ice.

again at the toe of the ice only a half mile away, forming concentric moraine ridges.

Below the moraine, other meltwater streams colored like weak milk tumble over rocky ledges to alpine meadows, where turf is swallowing glacial boulders. Smoothly fluted mounds of gray granitic rock crop up from the green carpet of alpine grasses. Rock panes—glacial polish—flash in the Sierra sun where bedrock was smoothed by the overriding ice. Thin scratches and deep grooves mar otherwise flat or billowy surfaces. These imperfections are the signatures of the glacier that once scraped the bedrock with loose rocks it dragged along its bed, grinding both large and small fragments against each other to produce floury granules, the same silt substance that colors the milky water now flowing past. An occasional metamorphic boulder, streaked or spotted reddish or dark-gray, perches atop a light granitic rock outcropping well above the level of today's streams, carried there on the ice from its parent bed high on a mountain summit.

Mount Lyell was a pivotal point during the main Ice Age, too: One ice stream started north

Tenaya Lake is crowned with domes: Polly Dome at left, Pywiack in low center, and Medlicott and others above. Beyond the domes is the valley down which flowed the lengthy Tuolumne Glacier. From that ice mass a lobe spilt through the gap into the foreground of this scene and passed down canyon to Yosemite Valley, there joining other ice tongues to shape that master-piece, too.

from the peak and then flowed westward to Hetch Hetchy Valley, its 60 miles making this the longest ancient glacier of the Sierra Nevada. At Tuolumne Meadows a major lobe from this glacier spilled down Tenaya Canyon and thence into Yosemite Valley. Another glacier stream started from the west and south sides of Mount Lyell to eventually join the lobe from the first at Yosemite Valley, this one reaching there by way of the Merced River's Nevada and Vernal Falls. A third glacier flowed east from near this same summit. Each quarried its headwall back as if to join the other glaciers that were eating into the cirque hollows on their sides of the peak, thus creating a "horn" peak, like Switzerland's Matterhorn.

There was action: rocks fell from summit ridges, rumbling out onto the ice; crevasses opened and closed with harsh cracks; ice blocks tumbled down icefalls, roaring.

Nearly all the High Sierra was covered with glaciers during the Ice Age, the ice rounding and polishing rock surfaces as it moved across them. Only higher peaks and ridges, including Mount

Lyell's summit, stood above the ice. At Tuolumne Meadows, taking the "ice line" as the boundary between the glacially smoothed lower slopes and the unglaciated steep, hackly upper ones on castellated summits such as Cathedral and Unicorn peaks, the glaciers were more than 2,000 feet thick! Lembert Dome and all the other domes at Tuolumne Meadows were repeatedly buried under ice.

The glacier lobes that branched into Yosemite Valley from Tuolumne Meadows flowed across a shallow divide, passing over the strong granitic rocks of Fairview, Medlicott, Pywiack, and Polly domes into a zone of fractured granitic rock, there quarrying out blocks to form the basin that is now Tenaya Lake. Also buried under the earlier ice flows were Moraine Dome in Little Yosemite Valley and North Dome at the head of Yosemite Valley. The polished bedrock canyons at Merced Lake on the upper Merced River and Pywiack Cascade in Tenaya Canyon below Clouds Rest were slippery glacier beds. But of course all of this landscape was not then visible; all these smoothed granite mounds, polished rock floors, strewn boulders and rock ridges, and lakes-to-be were below the ice, waiting for their place in the sun.

Glaciation of Yosemite's High Sierra was not a one-time thing; ice invasions occurred over a million-year span. The last ice advance (except for the small glaciers that have reformed in more recent time) peaked some 20,000 years ago. Finally the snow and ice ran out, and the glaciers stagnated. Slowly, as the ice masses melted and vanished, their burdens of rock fragments lowered to the ground and were left in rubbly piles. Occasionally the glacier snouts re-advanced slightly, pushing

died as boulders tumbled into canyon bottoms and streams carried silt into lakes. Living things then gained a foothold as this loose debris was achieving stability.

PLANTS IN A CHANGING LAND

During the Ice Age, when the climate of much of the world was cooler, many mountain plant species were forced several times to ever-lower elevations. Once below the cold, they spread laterally, colonizing the greater area available to them—such as the shores of lakes that had formed in the desert

JEFF GNASS

California Falls on the Tuolumne River tumbles down glacially smoothed granitic bedrock below Falls Ridge as it heads into the Grand Canyon of the Tuolumne River and its Muir Gorge. Earlier, the longest glacier of the Sierra Nevada followed this course and hollowed out Hetch Hetchy Valley— the "Tuolumne Yosemite."

KATHLEEN NORRIS COOK

up ridges. Meltwater coursed about among fields of ice and heaps of debris, washing away finer material and depositing and reworking gravels, but leaving the large boulders where they lay— where they still lie, as *glacial erratics*. Lakes were left where glaciers had gouged basins in the bedrock and ponds developed over isolated ice blocks as these melted under the landscape.

Geologically speaking, only a little time (some 15,000 years) has passed since the ice melted, and the evidence of the power of the glaciers is still very much part of the scene. In lower elevations, where the ice melted first, glacier trails are less obvious. Much softening of the glaciers' marks probably occurred just after the glaciers

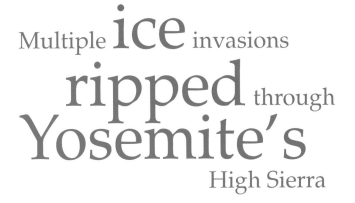

Multiple ice invasions ripped through Yosemite's High Sierra

of the Basin and Range Province, just east of Yosemite. Meanwhile, other plant species moved southward from the Arctic in front of the advancing continental glaciers, mixing with the species that had come down from the mountains.

DENNIS FLAHERTY

Young bighorn sheep perch on a boulder, at home in the park's craggy peaks and ridges. This "animal mountaineer" is at risk and once had disappeared completely from Yosemite. Now an attempt is being made to reestablish the species.

EDA ROGERS

You may hear a squeak before—if—you see this "rock-rabbit." The pika, or cony, lives in rock piles at higher altitudes.

When the climate warmed, some former mountain species migrated northward along with species that had come from there. And many former arctic species migrated upward into the High Sierra along with species that had originally descended from there. The most cold-tolerant became isolated together above treeline.

Thus, some of the same kinds of plants found today along the Arctic Ocean also grow stranded on high summits in Yosemite, as the plants can no longer migrate through the desert and forest habitats that separate these regions. Similarly, there are plants closely related to Yosemite's peak-top species in other regions of high mountains, such as Europe's Alps. Some colonies and even whole species may have vanished completely from lower summits as

FRANK S. BALTHIS

Not often seen, the marten is among Yosemite's wilderness creatures. The size of a large cat, it lives in the upper pine and fir forests, hunting for small mammals, insects, birds, fruits, and nuts.

the warming climate "pushed" their necessary environment upward off these mountaintops faster than they could adapt.

As plants returned to the High Sierra, they aided in the formation of soil. Lichens loosened individual crystals from solid rock; trees pried cracks apart with their expanding roots; sedges and grasses caught silt along stream and lake edges and held it in their roots to form turf that eventually became meadows and alpine rock gardens. Lodgepole pines and other trees from the forests below moved upward, climbing higher with each succeeding generation.

In Yosemite the treeline rose to 11,000 feet, where it is today. At this altitude, whitebark pines put forth tentative shoots into the persistent wind. But flying sand and ice trim away foliage on the windward side of the trunks, leaving only thin "flags" of foliage on the protected side.

The High Sierra has a *boreal*, or northern, climate. Snow buries much of the upper range for more than half the year, and in shaded areas of the highest regions it may not melt at all in summer. The very name of the range, the Spanish *Sierra Nevada* ("snowy mountain range"), reflects its character. Snow has been known to fall at a rate of five feet per day—up to ten feet can accumulate in weeklong storms. During such periods many trees are bent over by their snow burdens, and some

DENNIS FLAHERTY

Growing out of cracks in otherwise solid granitic rock, western junipers standing against the sky reveal in their bizarrely twisted and stunted forms the severity of their lives. Yet they survive—for a thousand years or more—and lend picturesque beauty to their home landscapes.

Winter Moods of Half Dome

TOM ALGIRE

DENNIS FLAHERTY

*M*any park visitors know the varying moods of Half Dome through the changing seasons of spring, summer, and fall. Even on similar winter days Half Dome's aspect can change with the shifting sunlight as frost melts in late dawn or colors change to gold in twilight. Much of Yosemite's appeal comes from the diversity the park displays. Devotees return again and again to enjoy familiar scenes, yet stay at the ready for chance encounters and observations, too. Serendipity is the name of this process—of being open to things not actively looked for. Nature has a way of providing the show.

Ragged Peak stands above one of the Young Lakes in *Yosemite's High Sierra. Many glacial lakes dot this region but the hackled upper slopes of this peak show it has always stood above the ice. This is wilderness, where hiking and backpacking prevail over mechanized travel.*

FRANK S. BALTHIS

GLENN VAN NIMWEGEN

Rock panes gleam in the *Sierra sun. Continuous when polished by the ice, pits have since weathered into this glacial polish.*

never straighten. Avalanches of snow race downslope, breaking trees and carrying them and other debris far out onto the meadows and frozen lakes.

Plants must do all their growing during summer, here a very short season. Near the glaciers the growing season is less than 60 days and is full of uncertainties: A midsummer night may be freezing cold, even though the day was uncomfortably hot (a result of intense solar radiation in the thin atmosphere). Often little or no rain falls from the end of May until October, so that once the snowmelt has run off, the crystalline soil becomes as arid as desert sand. Torrents of water from sudden cloudbursts may wash soil from tree roots and deposit gravel strips over the meadow grasses. Lightning may shatter trees and set them afire, and driving hail may shear blossoms from alpine flowers just when they are ready to be pollinated or produce seeds.

The sparse plants here respond in their own ways to such conditions. Most—such as the white heather, alpine willow, mountain sorrel, and draba—grow close to the ground, often in little cushions, to escape the wind that prevails only a few inches above. Many also grow hairs on their stems and leaves, an adaptation that retards evaporation of the scant moisture, as do some low-altitude desert plants that grow in similar aridity. Flowering plants burst forth in showy blossoms that attract insects and birds. Furthermore, the plants here are predominantly perennials—if they cannot reproduce one year, they still have a chance to do so the next!

ANIMALS OF THE HIGH COUNTRY

The first animals that returned to the region after the glaciers melted were probably insects, traveling on the wind. Even today dragonflies are found on the glaciers, blown there from elevations far below. Other insects arrived along with their host plants.

***H**ere is true High Sierra—where rocks are bare, trees are sparse, and the meadow grasses are still engulfing boulders dropped by glaciers. The dome, gleaming in the twilight, shows how the rock is casting off concentric layers, giving it its rounded form. Brilliant scenes like this inspired John Muir to call the Sierra Nevada the "Range of Light."*

One such "hitchhiker" is the lodgepole-pine needleminer, a little moth that while in larval stage utilizes only the needles of that one tree. This insect drills into the foliage for food and shelter, then emerges every odd-numbered year to fly in swarms, reproduce, deposit more eggs, and die.

This situation is an example of a natural balance. Man need not take sides either to aid the insects in their fight for survival or to try to eliminate them in order to help save the trees. At times so many larvae are at work that they kill their too-generous hosts, and the result is "ghost forests" of dead, bleaching trees that periodically develop throughout parts of the lodgepole range in the park. But the forest as a whole is not endangered. Needleminer outbreaks are spotty and last only a few to several years, until a cooler, rainy period occurs in which the moths fail to reproduce as effectively and the trees flourish again. Neither the needleminer nor the lodgepole pine seems likely to win this struggle; it merely continues.

Together with the insects came their predators,

birds. Mountain chickadees and flycatchers have a feast when the millions of needleminers hatch. Rosy finches, which take up summer residence on the permanent snowfields and glaciers, flit about eating hapless insects immobilized by the cold. Blue grouse are secure in their niche eating the food that is most abundant in these birds' area in winter as well as summer—needles from the fir trees. Clark's nutcrackers also live on tree food, tearing whitebark pinecones apart to get at the nuts inside. Most birds that come to the high country stay just for the summer, to mate and breed. The brightest of these are the crimson, yellow, and black male western tanagers. There are also mountain bluebirds, chickadees, great gray owls, eagles, and many more. Strange to see here are California gulls, so far from the sea—and the white pelican once found on Lyell Glacier must have been an even odder sight.

Mule deer presumably arrived soon after their shrubby forage plants became established. Today the region is crisscrossed with their migration trails. In years when winter hits suddenly with an

Pine seeds fall where they may—and then make the best of their situation. Like all others, this little tree requires sunlight, water, and nutrients, yet these are scarce at its rockbound site. To compensate the tree grows slowly, as a natural bonsai, and may be dozens of years old.

EDA ROGERS

Any fish that before the Ice Age lived in Yosemite's High Sierra were destroyed, along with their stream homes, by the grinding glaciers and the cold. After the ice melted, the water habitat that was left would have been suited to fish if not for the waterfalls that blocked upstream migration. In modern times trout were stocked in many park lakes and streams for anglers and some of these fish remain. But more than half the lakes in the park are fishless—protected places where native waterlife can live without being endangered by non-native trout, places where humans can watch and learn. Unfortunately, though, the frog populations of the park are in serious decline, a trend occurring in many parts of the United States, here partly due to the arrival of the non-native bullfrog.

Humans are little more than visitors in Yosemite's High Sierra. Yet the region exerts a strong appeal to many people, compelling them to return again and again. It has inspired fine literature—John Muir's *My First Summer in the Sierra*, for example— and excursions into its vastness served as one means for the early Sierra Club to rally members.

Every summer new enthusiasts discover the hundreds of miles of trails that access Yosemite's High Sierra, venturing forth to hike and backpack. Trail veterans return, too. Even so, and even today, in many parts of Yosemite's wilderness, a hiker can spend an entire day or longer without meeting another person. For purists, just the sign of one of their own species might spoil the wilderness experience. For them, there is one last wilderness left—the white wilderness of the cold months when all signs of people are covered. Not many take advantage of their privilege to experience this pristine world; a determined few slip quietly in on skis or tread on snowshoes over the crystalline snow and frozen lakes. Perhaps, for these few, even the solitude of nature in winter is not enough. Seeing the vast expanses of white and yearning also for the drama of action in their landscapes, they may imagine a time when the glaciers once again travel the High Sierra trails.

early-autumn snow, deer literally run to the west and downhill toward their winter grounds, lest they be caught in the high country for the winter and suffer certain death. Bighorn sheep came, too, to graze the higher slopes above the deer's normal range, but they winter on the east side of the Sierra. (Once gone from Yosemite, bighorns were reintroduced in 1986 but are not securely established.) Mountain lions followed the deer to prey on them, and although lion signs and tracks are frequently observed, sightings of the lions themselves are rare. Coyotes, foxes, and bobcats eat the rodents. Here, Nature operates by its own rules. We humans do not attempt to "tidy up" animals' situations to fit our notions, although effort is expended in keeping the animals' habitats wild, and in understanding and trying to deal with adverse effects (pollutants, non-native species, a few irresponsible park visitors) that drift into their range from outside the park's borders.

Many of the animals now living in the High Sierra seem to be too far south. The whitetail jackrabbit turns white in winter. The weasel in winter becomes the white ermine (of fur-coat fame, although not harvested here). Yellowbelly marmot and Belding ground squirrel ("picketpin" for its habit of standing upright by its burrow, like a stake placed to tether a horse or mule) hibernate beneath the snow. Marten, badger, porcupine, and pika are also residents.

SUGGESTED READING

McKenzie, Leonard. *in pictures Yosemite: The Continuing Story*. Wickenburg, Arizona: KC Publications, Inc., 1991.
Muir, John. *My First Summer in the Sierra*. Boston, Massachusetts: Houghton Mifflin, 1911.
O'Neill, Elizabeth Stone. *Meadow in the Sky: A History of Yosemite's Tuolumne Meadows Region*. Fresno, California: Panorama West Books, 1983.

T**his huge* glacial erratic ***boulder was left by a dying glacier to rest on bedrock smoothed by the same ice. Should you be fortunate enough to explore the High Sierra and find similar erratics, think of them as keys to understanding the region's glacial origin. Often the rock type of the glacial boulder differs from that of the bedrock it rests upon, but is the same as rock still in place elsewhere. Finding that bedrock gives a clue to the path the ice took and is a method geologists use to discover Yosemite's beginnings.

Tueeulala Falls leaps free 600 feet down a granitic rock cliff into Hetch Hetchy Valley, with a total descent from the rim of 1,000 feet. No meaning is known for the waterfall's name, said to be of Indian origin. A trail passes below the base of this little-known park waterfall, extending into park wilderness.

JOHN ELK III

Hetch Hetchy Valley lies inside Yosemite National Park 15 miles northwest of the much more famous Yosemite Valley, and has a striking resemblance. Each valley has the same style of cliff sculpture and similar granitic rocks. Hetch Hetchy Valley, too, has massive rock formations (Kolana Rock), waterfalls (Wapama and Tueeulala Falls), and domes (Hetch Hetchy Dome and others).

And each valley had glaciers that invaded a former stream canyon to widen it, although Hetch Hetchy's glaciers were longer and filled the valley completely. As a result, glacial polish is more obvious at Hetch Hetchy Valley, and moraines near it are more prominent than they are near Yosemite Valley.

But Yosemite Valley has been revered and Hetch Hetchy Valley has been dammed (some say damned). Although both have been included in the present park's area from its beginnings, a subsequent 1913 act of Congress gave San Francisco the right to develop Hetch Hetchy Valley for water and hydropower. Conservationists of the day were outraged, and the story is still a moving chapter in American environmental history. John Muir found "incredible" the damming of "one of Nature's rarest and most precious mountain temples."

Today at high water, the former Tuolumne River floods eight miles upstream from the dam. Many visitors are backpackers who enter the Yosemite wilderness here.

GAIL BANDINI

Hetch Hetchy Valley lies just northwest of its famous Yosemite Valley cousin and was formed in much the same way. But this valley was dammed and its former meadows and groves flooded. Tueeulala Falls drops to the left of the unnamed rock that looks like El Capitan reversed, and Wapama Falls comes down on the right.

Yosemite's three giant-sequoia groves contain trees that have stood since near the dawn of civilization and are among the world's largest living things.

Giant Sequoias – Life at Maximum

Giant sequoias are among the largest living things on earth. And they can live thousands of years. The formula by which specimen giant sequoias reach such great size and age is simple: They grow as long as they live, and they live a very long time. The species can be traced, through its fossils and those of its relatives, as far back as 200 million years, to a time when its ancestors, existing in a very similar form, forested much of the earth. For instance, huge giant sequoia stumps can be seen at Florissant National Monument in Colorado and on an Alaskan Aleutian Island beach.

Today the giant sequoia is truly a relict species, occurring only in isolated groves on the western slope of California's Sierra Nevada. Even though the species currently has a restricted natural range, the trees are healthy and can reproduce adequately. Why these trees are confined to isolated groves, then, is a mystery, for there is much more area available with what appears to be the same environment. Yet not even single trees are found naturally outside the boundaries of the groves, although some giant sequoias have been successfully propagated in other Yosemite sites such as Wawona and Yosemite Valley. Giant sequoia trees are growing at many other places including Sacramento (California), Reno (Nevada), and Europe.

For trees *age, girth, height,* and *bulk* are components of life at maximum.

Estimates of the *age* to which a giant sequoia may live vary widely, but tree-ring analysis shows they can reach at least 3,266 years. The alerce tree of Chile and Argentina, about as big around but not as tall as the giant sequoia, lives longer, at least to 3,613 years. Bristlecone pines may live longer still, up to 4,767 years; quite unlike the stately giant sequoia, at Yosemite these bizarrely twisted and stunted pines live at treeline, rarely attaining a height of over 50 feet.

As to *girth,* the trunk of the Grizzly Giant of Yosemite's Mariposa Grove tapers from 29 feet around near its base to 14 feet around at a height of 96 feet above ground, where its first large limb sprouts, a limb that itself is 6 feet in diameter, bigger across than most trees' trunks. The tule cypress grows thicker, but not as tall.

For *height,* the giant sequoia grows to over 300 feet, but the coast redwood—the world's tallest tree—can reach over 350 feet. Once the giant sequoia has reached its mature height, its growth is outward, giving older sequoias a bulbous form. Too, its height is limited by lightning strikes, common in the giant sequoia's Sierra, but rare in the coast redwood's range. Severe fire can also limit each species.

Egg-shaped cones from giant sequoia trees litter the forest floor. Each carries seeds that could start hundreds of new giants.

FRANK S. BALTHIS

The log cabin museum in Mariposa Grove gives scale to the immense volume and great tallness of nearby giant sequoia trees. Winter snows here are often many feet deep, discouraging entry except by skiers and snowshoers, but providing opportunity to experience this forest of massive trees with tranquility. Even in summer, access to the upper portion of the grove is by tram or walking, making the grove a special place to experience Nature at its grandest.

Try looking at Nature's marvels *from unusual angles! Lie on your back and gaze upward along red-barked giant sequoia trunk shafts. Watch scudding clouds drift over bulbous green treetops against the blue of the sky. Take time to pause and let the Yosemite world entertain you.*

JEFF GNASS

Sheer *bulk* gives the giant sequoia its main edge over other tree competitors. Sizes of trees can be computed on the basis of trunk volume. Factoring girth with height, Yosemite's Grizzly Giant sequoia tree, for instance, has a volume of more than 34,000 cubic feet. (The largest giant sequoia, the General Sherman Tree of Sequoia National Park, bulks over 52,500 feet!) Cloned aspens have immeasurable bulk, but with many single, smaller, shorter trunks coming up from wide-spreading root runners.

Combining age, girth, height, and bulk, the giant sequoia deserves the title for a tree of life at maximum!

REDWOOD AND REDWOOD

California has two trees that are sometimes both called, loosely, redwood. This is confusing. One tree is the giant sequoia (*Sequoiadendron giganteum*), also called Sierra redwood and bigtree, which grows only in the sunny and snowy Sierra Nevada as at Yosemite and Sequoia National Parks. The other is the coast redwood (*Sequoia sempervirens*), which grows only in fogbound coastal areas on the opposite side of the state such as at Muir Woods National Monument and Redwood National Park. Both trees have great girths and grow tall and live long, but their foliage and cones are different enough to place them in separate genera (*Sequoiadendron* versus *Sequoia*). Both trees have bark and heartwood of a red color, whence their names, although the giant sequoia's bark is cinnamon-colored whereas the coast redwood's bark is grayish-red. It does seem odd that the two princi-

Did fire "damage" this tree? Fire has eaten away much of this tree's supporting heartwood, rendering it much more vulnerable to collapse. Even sequoia trees are not invincible. But this Clothespin Tree has mocked an old-fashioned version of its namesake for more than a century and stands still. Peculiar shapes of "specimen" trees have given rise to descriptive names like Telescope Tree, Corridor Tree, and Faithful Couple. These add intrigue to the giant sequoia groves, further inspiring humans to continue preserving them in parks so future generations can marvel, too.

pal remnants of a family of huge trees once wide-spread throughout the world have retreated to mountains on opposite sides of California, separated by its Central Valley.

SURVIVING AGAINST THE ODDS

The Grizzly Giant has been standing for 1,800 years. This tree makes a great lightning target, and in one storm alone (1942) it was hit six times. During the long years of its existence it must have seen many thousands of storms and accepted countless bolts in its upper branches and top, possibly reducing its height. Today the tree is 209 feet tall. Its upward growth may also have been limited by fire that gnawed into its base, consuming sapwood and reducing the tree's vigor yet leaving it viable although scarred.

The first photograph of this tree, taken more than a century ago, showed it leaning at 17 degrees, and there has long been concern that it might fall. But today it still leans at the same angle, its bulk somehow balanced on its widely spreading but shallow root pad. (Trees only grow straight up; what caused this tree to lean?)

The Grizzly Giant will not die except through an extraordinary event, for its species has developed adaptations that make it highly resistant to most attackers, including insects and fungi. Perhaps, as did Mariposa Grove's road-spanning Wawona Tunnel Tree in 1969, it will fall during a record snowfall, when the crushing weight of snow overloads its branches and causes an imbalance.

Or perhaps a particularly violent lightning bolt will shatter its trunk or burn its life-supporting cambium to the point that it can no longer survive.

Or the soil around its root base may become so water-saturated and mushy on the leaning side that it can no longer support the huge tree in its less-than-upright position.

This giant has persisted through many stresses

A chickaree or Douglas squirrel rides a high branch in its treetop home against the clear blue sky. Chattering among themselves or at any intruder, this tree squirrel cuts evergreen cones from tree branches or shucks scales from cones to scatter in "midden" piles below. It's a charmer with dashing antics.

EDA ROGERS

in its vast lifetime—even the threat of being cut down for lumber or display before it was protected within a national park. Thus nature alone will likely cause its death. Such a death is not something one likes to contemplate, but it is a thrill to imagine the earthshaking, reverberating boom that this giant will make as, reacting to some incredible strain, its 2 million pounds crash to earth—a venerable, noble giant at last relinquishing its tenacious hold on life!

THE YOSEMITE SEQUOIA GROVES

Yosemite has 3 giant-sequoia groves. Mariposa Grove lies south of Yosemite Valley; it is the best known and most visited. Merced and Tuolumne groves lie north of Yosemite Valley. (Sequoia and Kings Canyon National Parks, south of Yosemite, contain 30 groves, and others are in national forests and state parks.) Major parts of all 3 Yosemite groves are accessible only to hikers, and so it is possible to find near-solitude under the ancient columns and to spend time well in reflection and contemplation.

Elevations in Yosemite's groves range from 5,200 feet in the Merced Grove to 6,800 feet in the upper Mariposa Grove. Usual climates in the groves are warm, generally dry summers and sunny winters interrupted by infrequent snowstorms that may last a day or a week, leaving several feet of new snow—or just a trace. High winds occur but are not frequent where sequoias grow, but thunderstorms with lightning bolts are common.

REPRODUCTION AND GROWTH

The maturity of a giant sequoia is not necessarily indicated by hugeness, for the tree begins to produce cones with viable seeds after only a few years of life. When at full size, sequoias generate about 600 new cones every year, each cone containing a few hundred healthy seeds, so that these bigger trees produce more than 100,000 seeds annually. The average larger sequoia holds 10,000 cones in its branches, with perhaps 2 million seeds inside them; and the hugest sequoias may bear as many as 40,000 cones (as many as 8 million seeds). The large, old trees therefore have the best chance of successfully propagating their genetic character.

But the cones do not just fall off the trees and release the seeds. This is done in part by an unknowing agent—the chickaree, or Douglas squirrel. This little tree squirrel relishes the fleshy scales of the sequoia cones, and as it feasts on them, the seeds, largely ignored by the busy diner, scatter on the forest floor. A single animal has been known to cut cones at a rate of more than 500 in half an hour, and several thousand in a season! Another agent is an insect borer—a beetle—that bores the cones, causing them to dry and then fall to the ground.

Once the seeds reach the forest floor, if they come to rest on a thick duff of needles and twigs, reproduction fails. Sunlight and nourishment, in the forms of moisture and the minerals of bare soil, must be present. Fires, by clearing the forest floor, encourage such conditions.

Of course, in fires the seeds that already lie on the ground are burned. So nature ensures reproduction of the giant sequoia another way: heat from fires rises into the tree's branches and dries the cones. A day or so after a fire, the cones open and release their seeds, which fall on the cooling ashes below. With fortuitous rainfall, in a few months tiny sequoia seedlings protrude from the bare soil, vying for the honor of a place beside their giant parents. Most of the seedlings will die, of course, but if only one offspring of a mature giant sequoia is successful during the parent tree's long life-span, the population count of this tree will remain constant.

FIRE: FOE OR FRIEND?

"Of all living things," wrote one admirer, "only the giant sequoia is assured of living long enough to be struck by lightning." Thus it is that nearly every mature giant sequoia bears the scars of lightning-caused fires, some of which are extensive. But even the most severe burn damage may not destroy this tree, with its incredible ability to survive.

Fire is a force of nature. For millennia fires—caused by lightning or purposely set by Native Americans—ran through the forests of Yosemite National Park and the Sierra Nevada. Because these ancient fires were frequent, underbrush, fallen branches, and logs were consumed at intervals so that fires were generally light. Mature, bark-protected trees were mainly left intact. With establishment of the park, the attempt became to suppress all fires to "protect" the trees. During the century plus of this approach, forest fuel became more abundant and some wildfires today have become absolute conflagrations. As a result, fire policy has evolved again. Today park and forest managers prescribe burning under favorable conditions to simulate nature's effect. Some naturally-started fires are allowed to burn their course. Yet until the forests can be returned to a state with less fuel, major or threatening fires will continue to be suppressed.

[Note: Yosemite National Park has taken a lead in reassessing fire management policy and gaining public understanding of the new approach. We as author and publisher of Yosemite: The Story Behind the Scenery *are proud to have explained that effort in our first, 1971, edition.]* K.C. DENDOOVEN, PUBLISHER

Forest managers have long known that fire is requisite to certain kinds of plant life; however, it is only in recent years that this natural law has begun to be understood by the public. Virtually all of the specimen trees in the groves show fire scars on their trunks. (Studies of annual tree rings show that the Mariposa Grove has burned on average every 20 to 25 years.) Dry sequoia heartwood burns well, but the mature tree's highly insulating bark— which may be as thick as 18 inches—retards fire.

Summer and autumn fires are part of the natural environment in which the giant sequoias live. Mature sugar and yellow pines that live together with the giant sequoia in the mixed-conifer forests of the Sierra Nevada rely, too, on these occasional fires for their existence. Without fire to clear out the limb canopy overhead, sunlight would not pene-

*T*runs of a huge ponderosa pine—with "alligator" bark—and a comparably large but thickly branched incense-cedar shoot for the sky. These two tree species are widespread in the mid-altitude Sierra Nevada forests including Yosemite Valley and are also companions to the giant sequoias in the restricted groves that tree occupies.

young seedlings, delicate and spindly-leafed, look as if they are hardly capable of growing to the monstrous sizes that their adult relatives have attained.

New Concepts of Conservation

For many years a policy of excluding all fire from the Sierra Nevada forests was followed. The fuels that then accumulated could easily have fed an uncontrollable conflagration wherein fire, leaping swiftly to and across tree crowns, could devastate an entire forest, certainly not nature's way in the Sierra Nevada. Because of improved understanding of how fires behave and new and better methods to manage them, park foresters have changed their approach. In some areas "prescribed" fires are being set in the groves and surrounding mixed-conifer forests to return them to the natural conditions that existed a century and more ago when lighter fires ran through the woods every few decades, burning the accumulated fallen limbs and pine needles so that no great buildup of fuel occurred.

Over a century ago John Muir described the "varied beauty of fire effects" as he watched in a giant sequoia forest:

> *Fire grazing, nibbling on the floor... spinning into thousands of little jets—lamps of pure flame...old prostrate trunks glowing like red-hot bars.... Smoke and showers of white, fluffy ashes from the fire boring out trunks, rills of violet fire running up the furrows swiftly, lighting huge torches flaming overhead two hundred feet...burning with fierce fateful roar and stormy booming...black and lurid smoke surges steaming through the trees, the columns of which look like masts of ships obscured in scud and flying clouds.*

And so, fire is another of the numerous elements of the environment that this ancient giant species has adapted to in its successful spanning of millennia. Is it possible that the longevity of the giant sequoia and its gigantism serve to eliminate its vulnerability to the short climatic/environmental

trate to the offspring of these sun-loving trees, and their seeds would either not sprout or their seedlings would languish in the shadows below. The forests would fill instead with shade-tolerant white fir and incense-cedar.

Although fires have certainly caused great injury to some giant sequoia trees, burning them through and even killing some, fires have also created some spectacular, still-living shells—a source of amazement. Curious people come to marvel at oddities such as the Corridor Tree (with multiple support columns around a hollowed-out base), the Telescope Tree (from inside you see sky out its top), and the Clothespin Tree (shaped like an old-fashioned version of its namesake with a long hollow slot between its two legs).

"Specimen" trees are the most dramatic features of the giant-sequoia groves; even so, one can easily become engrossed in studying other aspects of this wonderful tree—its life cycle, for example. The

"Black" bears (usually brown in Yosemite) may prowl any time of year in the lower forests, denning only when food is scarce, snow is deep, or they are giving birth. Grizzly bears have disappeared from the park and from California.

DICK DIETRICH

swings that seem to affect other species—including humans—so profoundly? Perhaps that is the purpose and value of these characteristics that to us are so marvelous.

SUGGESTED READING

DE GOLIA, JACK. *Fire—A Force of Nature: The Story Behind the Scenery*. Wickenburg, Arizona: KC Publications, 1989.

HARVEY, H. THOMAS. *Sequoias of Yosemite National Park*. Yosemite, California: Yosemite Association, 1988.

MUIR, JOHN. *Sierra Big Trees*. Reprint. Silverthorne, Colorado: VistaBooks, 1980.

PARUK, JIM. *Sierra Nevada Tree Identifier*. Yosemite, California: Yosemite Association, 1998.

WILLARD, DWIGHT. *A Guide to the Sequoia Groves of California*. Yosemite, California: Yosemite Association, 2000.

FRED HIRSCHMANN

Between Yosemite Valley and the Mariposa Grove lies the valley of Wawona, and standing above is Wawona Dome, another example of exfoliating granitic rock. This area is sometimes called a "half Yosemite," for its formations are all on one side of the valley.

The appeal of Yosemite commanded notice—in establishment of what is arguably the world's first national park.

Before There Was a Park

TOM MYERS

Yosemite has been home to Native Americans for thousands of years. The latest have been Miwok Indians, who hunted animals and gathered seeds to make their living. In this reenactment, acorn bread is being cooked on hot rocks. The Miwok had a clan social structure and their legends explained the valley's formation to them, often emphasizing wild animals or human behavior.

TOM ALGIRE

During the Ice Age, people made their way into North America and rapidly dispersed into their new continent. Early transients might have seen Yosemite Valley when it was still being gouged by a glacier or when it held its ancient lake. By 4,000 years ago Indians had settled in Yosemite, giving them an occupation span at least 25 times as long as modern people. Traces they left include arrowheads, bowl-shaped grinding holes in flat-topped boulders, and weathered rock markings. These Indians lived close to nature, harvesting some of its bounty to meet their own needs, and trading with adjacent tribes.

The relationship between the American Indian and nature was, in fact, inspiration that contributed to the first proposal for a national park, made almost 40 years before the idea was realized. Indian painter and explorer George Catlin, in an 1833 New York newspaper, proposed:

A *rare fog shrouds the forests and meadows of Yosemite Valley on a winter day, giving the scene a whole new aspect and showing another of Yosemite's many moods. The cliffs and falls stand forth as always, but the valley floor takes on an appearance somewhat like we may imagine Lake Yosemite to have had. El Capitan is the tall cliff on the left; Half Dome is obvious; Bridalveil Fall drops in.*

A nation's park, containing man and beast, in all the wild and freshness of their nature's beauty... where the world could see for ages to come, the native Indian in his classic attire, galloping his wild horse... amid the fleeting herds of elks and buffaloes.

By coincidence, Catlin's vision was made public the same year non-Indians first entered the area that is now Yosemite National Park. Traveling west along the Indians' Mono Trail, a portion of which is now the route of the Tioga Road, Joseph Walker and his party of trappers probably "discovered"

Interdenominational Yosemite
Chapel dates from 1879, and is
the oldest structure still in use in Yosemite.
What a place to worship amid nature's glory!

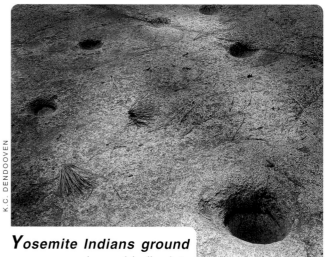

Yosemite Indians ground
acorns, seeds, and bulbs into
flour on flat-topped boulders, in time wearing
deep mortar holes with stone pestles.

(for their culture) the Yosemite Valley, from its rim; the giant sequoias; and the High Sierra. These men were looking for beaver pelts to sell to Eastern and European fur hat markets but must have been disappointed because beaver is alien to this part of the mountains; they made little report of the scenery.

GOLD FEVER AND STRIFE

The Walker party had likely been observed by the Indians, but life in Yosemite remained much as before until 1848. Then an event occurred some 100 miles to the north that would affect not only the Yosemite Indians, but the entire region, nation, and world. In a foothill stream, deposited there eons before following its erosion from the bedrock of the central Sierra Nevada, a discovery was made: *gold!*

Explorer Kit Carson soon traced this placer gold to its source, discovering the first lode gold on John Fremont's newly acquired estate west of Yosemite. Interest in the entire Mother Lode foothills region exploded, and "49er" prospectors swarmed in.

The man who figured most pivotally in this chapter of Yosemite's history was a real frontiersman. James Savage had been a foothill trader before gold was discovered. His relations with the Indians had been good (he had married into five tribes). With the gold rush his business profited; both Indian and white miners came to his stores to obtain supplies. Prices, however, were set high (one trader is said to have charged one pound of gold for a hat!). Merchants made more by "mining" the miners than most miners did mining the mines.

Miners spread operations over the foothills and established booming towns. A few of them lifted their eyes to gaze upon the magnificent peaks of the High Sierra. Some wrote down their impressions, but these observations went largely unnoticed. It was gold, not scenery, that was the issue of the day!

The Indians, watching miners, became apprehensive. The two sides clashed over territory, property, and rights. The native people perceived a threat—surely they would suffer as this new society settled on lands the Indians had traditionally used for hunting and other food gathering.

And so the Indians determined to drive the miners out. Their first attack was on Savage's South Fork station on the Merced River below Yosemite Valley. The miners retaliated, deciding for their part that the Indians must be driven from the mountains to reservations in the San Joaquin Valley. Thus began the Mariposa Indian War.

James Savage joined the Mariposa Battalion of volunteers. The amateur soldiers soon headed for the home of the band they thought had raided South Fork Station. This group became the first other than Indians to enter Yosemite Valley. Their

Skeleton of a once-vibrant Jeffrey pine that sprouted from a crack atop Sentinel Dome, above the south rim of Yosemite Valley. Popular with tree climbers in spite of advice to the contrary, the tree's overuse may have killed it. Views from the dome's summit are 360 degrees—east to the Sierra crest, west to the Central Valley, and into Yosemite Valley below.

FRED HIRSCHMANN

purpose was not discovery: they were to capture Indians. But it was snowing; the river was high, cold, and hard to ford; and they couldn't even find their quarry. "It's a hell of a place" was Savage's succinct comment about Yosemite.

In spite of the hardships, at least one man in the party was enthusiastic about the marvelous valley. Dr. Lafayette Bunnell, a physician, proposed at the campfire on the first night in the valley that the valley be named for its Indian inhabitants—known to the soldiers by the name Yosemite—the very tribe they hoped to remove! (The Indians, on the other hand, called their valley *Ahwahnee*.)

And so the valley became known to this society using a written language, yet for another four years no adequate description reached the outside world. When it did, the valley's fame spread rapidly. Writers, artists, and photographers came to see the area and give to the world the creations of their minds and hearts that this wondrous place inspired.

THE CAUSE FOR CONSERVATION

In spite of all the publicity about this new western paradise, no one at first thought about preserving it. Perhaps Horace Greeley, editor of New York's *Tribune*, was the first to espouse the cause of protection for Yosemite. In 1859, inspired by the giant sequoias of the Mariposa Grove, he wrote:

If the village of Mariposas, the county, or the State of California, does not immediately provide for the safety of these trees, I shall deeply deplore the infatuation and believe that these giants might have been more happily located.

Still nothing happened to preserve the area. Then, in 1862, an incident of nature occurred that was to awaken the entire world to the need for preservation of natural areas. In that year more than 100 inches of rain fell on the Sierra Nevada within a three-month period, generating a disastrous flood that crippled the transportation system of the whole state and inundated the gold mines on John Fremont's rich Mariposa Grant just west of Yosemite, a factor contributing to its bankruptcy.

It happened that Frederick Law Olmsted, who designed New York's Central Park, was then "on strike," having disagreed over a matter of principle with that park's founders. Fremont's New York creditors were thus able to hire Olmsted to superintend their newly acquired mines in far-off California.

About then a bogus lottery was attempted. In this uncompleted scheme the whole of the valley was to be "raffled away" at a dollar a chance. Olmsted, arriving in September 1863, got behind the drive for a park. Legislation soon cleared Congress, and Abraham Lincoln signed the

JEFF GNASS

It was during one of the darkest hours, before Sherman had begun the march upon Atlanta or Grant his terrible movement through the Wilderness, when the paintings of Bierstadt and the photographs of Watkins, both productions of the war time, had given to the people on the Atlantic some idea of the sublimity of the Yosemite, and of the stateliness of the neighboring Sequoia Grove, that consideration was first given to the danger that such scenes might become private property and through the false taste, caprice or the requirements of some industrial speculation of their holders, their value to posterity be injured.

Today Olmsted's work is remembered at Frederick Law Olmsted National Historic Park in Massachusetts and at Olmsted Point on Yosemite's Tioga Road overlooking Tenaya Lake. Those involved in park planning today, a major effort now, consider him the "father of landscape architecture."

THE FIRST NATIONAL PARK?

And so the national park idea became established. Today it is Yellowstone that is officially recognized as our first national park, having been created in 1872, but the writers and park managers of the 1860s thought of Yosemite as the first.

That Yosemite was meant to be considered a *national* resource, even though it was at first state-controlled, is borne out in statements by Olmsted. In an 1865 report Olmsted recommended how to manage the grant and stressed its national importance:

"It is the will of the nation that this scenery ... shall be held solely for public purposes."

State Geologist Josiah Whitney (for whom Mount Whitney is named), on the board of commissioners with Olmsted, agreed. Whitney was the first to use the phrase *national park*, applying it in 1868 to Yosemite.

At that time the park had but two smaller, separate pieces—the Yosemite Valley and the Mariposa Grove of Giant Sequoias. The watershed for the famous falls was being grazed by sheep, and the High Sierra was open to homesteading and mining

"Yosemite Grant" into law on June 30, 1864. Few parks have had a shorter enactment period.

The grant language was profound and a precursor to similar language to be used later in the establishment of other parks. The grant gave

...to the State of California the 'cleft' or 'gorge' in the granite peak of the Sierra Nevada Mountains...known as the Yo-Semite Valley...upon the express conditions that the premises shall be held for public use, resort, and recreation; shall be inalienable for all time.

The grant included the Mariposa Big Tree Grove for the same purposes.

Olmsted became chairman of the first board of commissioners (all appointed by the state governor and all non-paid) to manage the Yosemite Grant. Soon he had a "master plan" for the area. In his plan he philosophized about how the Civil War may have been the significant event that alerted the American people to the need to care for and preserve areas of unusual beauty for public use:

claims. Overgrazing was severe. In 1870 an astute observer, Professor Joseph LeConte of the University of California, recorded some 12,000 to 15,000 sheep in Tuolumne Meadows alone! There were even threats of water development projects.

Fortunately, conservationists of the day rallied to correct the situation. Even more fortunately, they had an eloquent spokesman in John Muir. Muir was new to California; he had not arrived until 1868, and then spent his first year overseeing the herding of sheep in Yosemite's high pastures. His firsthand experiences instilled in him deep appreciation for Yosemite and the threats to it. He began writing for Eastern magazines. It was he who coined the term "hoofed locusts" for the woolly bundles of sheep devastating the high meadows. When his publisher suggested launching a campaign to enlarge the park, Muir was immediately receptive.

Success was realized with legislation in 1890, when lands surrounding Yosemite Valley and the Mariposa Grove were added, giving the park substantially its present size, although some reductions occurred soon after to provide for timber, mineral, grazing, and water interests. These reductions would certainly have grown throughout the years had it not been for the efforts of Muir and a group largely of university and other professional people who foresaw that encroachment would continue if not met with solid resistance. Thus it was that in 1892 the Sierra Club was formed, with John Muir as its first president.

The step remaining was to place all parts of the park under one administration, the federal government. (Up to that time, the park area had been administered by two entities: Yosemite Valley and the Mariposa Grove had remained under state management, and the surrounding area was administered by the Department of the Interior, which detailed army troops there for patrolling it.) Action to accomplish this was started in 1903 by President Theodore Roosevelt following a camping trip to Glacier Point, a trip on which he was accompanied by Muir, the most persuasive supporter the park could have had. In 1906 the valley and Mariposa Grove were receded to the federal government and incorporated into the surrounding national park.

And so it is that Muir is called "the father of Yosemite National Park." Even though the initial park area was established several years before he first saw it and long before he began to work actively in its behalf, the accolade fits: Muir has been at least as influential in the development of the park idea as those who conceived it. His influence

The Father of Yosemite National Park

NPS PHOTO

John Muir, eminent 19th-century naturalist, lived in Yosemite many years. His tireless work and eloquent writings in its behalf give him the title "father of Yosemite National Park."

was felt in the legislative and executive halls of government. His prolific writings on Yosemite and other national parks made an important contribution to conservation not only in his day, but again today as the nation—and the world—renews environmental emphasis.

SUGGESTED READING

BATES, CRAIG D., and MARTHA J. LEE. *Tradition and Innovation: A Basket History of the Indians of the Yosemite-Mono Lake Area*. Yosemite, California: Yosemite Association, 1990.

HUTH, HANS. *Nature and the American: Three Centuries of Changing Attitudes*. Lincoln: University of Nebraska Press, 1990.

JOHNSTON, HANK. *The Yosemite Grant, 1864-1906: A Pictorial History*. Yosemite, California: Yosemite Association, 1995.

MUIR, JOHN. *The Proposed Yosemite National Park— Treasures and Features*. Reprint. Silverthorne, Colorado: VistaBooks, 1986.

RUSSELL, CARL P. *One Hundred Years in Yosemite*. Yosemite, California: Yosemite Association, 1992.

SANBORN, MARGARET. *Yosemite: Its Discovery, Its Wonders and Its People*. Yosemite, California: Yosemite Association, 1989.

SUGGESTED DVD

Discovering Yosemite, DVD #DV-3, 2 Disc Set, 145 minutes, Whittier, California: Finley-Holiday Films.

Yosemite is the heart and soul of the mighty Sierra Nevada. Here, superlatives abound. Yosemite is a place to be enjoyed and kept intact— now and for the future.

Being at Yosemite

YOSEMITE CONCESSION SERVICES CORPORATION

At Yosemite, America's "love affair" with the automobile is being challenged. New forms of transport reduce noise, traffic, and pollution, with the intent of restoring quality to park visits. Increasingly, cars are parked in the valley or even before arrival, and driving chores are left to others.

Yosemite has world-class waterfalls for gazing. At least it has them in spring and early summer when snows melt from the high country and the released water rushes toward the valley's brinks. In late summer, however, waterfalls like this Lower Yosemite Fall run nearly or completely dry and then one's gaze turns to the massive cliffs. An ambitious hike leads to an overlook near the top of Upper Yosemite Fall, half a mile vertically up. There are even ledges and walls that climbers explore in between. Yosemite activities can be passive, mild, moderate, or extreme.

Yosemite Is

...a geologic wonder, a raucous Steller's jay, a swaying waterfall, a blade of frosted meadow grass, half a dome, a doe with spotted fawn, white dogwood blossoms, a mountain lake, a pine-bough campfire, a yodel from a peak.

...a skyful of swirling snowflakes, the prose of John Muir, a sandy beach, a smoky forest fire, a dying glacier, a tawny mountain lion, a blooming azalea, a cliff-side trail, a mosquito's buzz and bite, a study in granites.

...a marmot on a rock, fringed gentian abloom in late summer, a sheer cliff, a polished rock slab, ice crystals ringing a streambed boulder, dew on a spider's web, a hard hike, a park ranger on a horse, sliding on skis across a frozen lake.

...a sparkling cascade, smelly wild onions, a rosy finch on a summer snowbank, a two-foot-long sugar pinecone, acorns under valley oaks, a river pool, immense and old giant sequoia trees, tiny giant sequoia cones.

...sawtooth ridges to scramble along, crystal knobs sticking out from granitic rocks, rumbling rockfalls, charred forest trees, barren avalanche tracks, golden aspen leaves.

YOSEMITE IS still more.

High Sierra skyline looms above Tuolumne Meadows from atop Lembert Dome. In view are peaks to climb, trails to hike, meadows to roam, photos to be taken. Summer days may be cloud-free or packed with billowing thunderheads punctuated with lightning flashes. You won't be bored.

Winter on the Valley rim at Dewey Point gives another portrayal of Yosemite's diversity. Snows may pile ten feet deep in the high country and last well into June, but ski and snowshoe trails explore the region, and there are backcountry shelters.

PENNY KERR

*T*ravel into the park's wilderness western style, on horseback. Trips to mountain meadows, high-country lakes, across windy passes, and along rushing streams can be taken. Single-day, overnight, and weeklong trips are possible. Park rangers still patrol trails using horses, just as the black "Buffalo Soldiers" of the U.S. Cavalry did when it ran the park in its earliest days.

JOHN ELK III

*S*hadows lengthen as the sun sets on two hikers perched atop Sentinel Dome above Yosemite Valley. Watching the orange disk of the sun settle in increments to finally drop below the horizon is one of the simple joys Yosemite can provide. Make such opportunities happen during your visit. You, too, will likely find peace and pleasure.

Sorting of ropes, rock hardware, carabiners, clothing, and food supplies precedes an attempt to ascend El Capitan, looming over the trees. Because of Yosemite Valley's steep walls that are thousands of feet tall and its massive granitic rocks, climbs here are world-class. The valley, especially, is a mecca for mountaineers the world over and has become a locus for development of climbing equipment and technique as well as climbers. High Sierra peaks draw interest, too, and there are ice fields to ascend as well. Instruction and guides are available at park climbing centers.

Bicycle paths on the floor of Yosemite Valley provide a way to view its rock formations, waterfalls, and open meadows without the distraction of driving. Bike riding gives a better chance of seeing animals, such as deer, and special birds. Rentals are available or BYOB— bring your own bike.

***F**loating down the Merced River offers* expansive views of Upper Yosemite Fall and other famous valley features. To protect the riverbank from excessive use, however, only certain sections of the river may be floated at certain water levels.

Yosemite National Park is the size of a small state, and is mostly wilderness. The best way to see such a natural masterpiece is by walking. The park has over 800 miles of trails, and marked over-snow trails as well. In turn, this trail land is adjoined in the Sierra Nevada by a stretch of wilderness that is longer than any other in the country outside Alaska.

Sitting works, too, at the right spots. Time and attention are needed to discover cliff details and be able to describe the behavior of something as seemingly simple as falling water. The animals will come forth in curiosity or indifference to quiet observers. John Muir discovered many of Yosemite's wonders by going out and sitting on the rocks. "Nature's peace will flow into you," he said, "While cares will drop off like autumn leaves."

JEFF GNASS

A *ramble along the crystal banks of the Tuolumne River entertains with sliding water chutes, foaming cascades, rippling pools. Bumpy rocks in the river are of Cathedral Peak Granite, pieces of which are found in Yosemite Valley, carried there by glaciers.*

All About Yosemite National Park

Yosemite Conservancy

In 2010 the Yosemite Association and The Yosemite Fund merged to form the Yosemite Conservancy.

The **Yosemite Association** was founded in 1923 as the Yosemite Natural History Association, a non-profit organization. Through a program of visitor services, publications, membership activities, and the publication and sale of literature and interpretive items, the Association provided over $300,000 annually to the park's visitor information, educational, and interpretive programs. The Association also organized volunteers to work on meadow, trail and other much-needed park restoration projects. In addition, it conducted over 60 outdoor classes on natural history, Native American lifeways, art and photography.

The Association operated and/or sponsored the Ostrander Ski Hut, Art Activity Center, and other valuable programs.

Providing for Yosemite is the Conservancy's passion. We inspire people to support projects and programs that preserve and protect Yosemite National Park's resources and enrich the visitor experience. The Yosemite Conservancy will ensure that Yosemite remains an irreplaceable resource and wondrous icon by funding projects and programs that provide a margin of excellence and future generations.

COMMON RAVEN
BY FRANK S. BALTHIS

The Yosemite Conservancy is now the only philanthropic organization dedicated exclusively to the protection and preservation of Yosemite National Park and the enhancement of the visitor experience. We are committed to creating unique opportunities for people to connect with the park. With more than 100 years of combined experience, we will continue making a difference for Yosemite's future.

The **Yosemite Fund**, also a non-profit organization, was started in 1988. It raised money from Yosemite enthusiasts to protect and restore the park and enhance visitors experience. The Fund distributed over $13 million for more than 150 projects. These included more than 2,000 bear-proof food lockers, rehabilitation of Cook's Meadow and trail rebuilding.

To contact the **Yosemite Conservancy:** PO. Box 230 El Portal, CA 95318 Phone: (209) 379-2317 Email: Info@YosemiteConservancy.Org

---

CONTACT INFO:

Call the park at:

(209) 372-0200.

Write to:

Superintendent
P.O. Box 577
Yosemite NP, CA 95389

Visit **the park's web site at:**

www.nps.gov/yose

Camping at the park:

(877) 444-6777

www.reservations.nps.gov

Lodging at the park:

Yosemite Concession Services Corporation

(559) 252-4848

www.yosemitepark.com

For public transportation at Yosemite:

Yosemite Area Regional Transportation System, YARTS

(800) 877-98YARTS

www.yarts.com

The Yosemite Institute

The Yosemite Institute is a private non-profit organization dedicated to providing educational adventures in nature's classroom to inspire a personal connection to the natural world and responsible actions to sustain it.

For over 30 years, Yosemite National Institutes has served over 40,000 youth and adults annually through a unique variety of environmental education programs at our national park campuses in California and Washington.

Contact Yosemite National Institute, P.O. Box 487, Yosemite, CA 95389; phone: (209) 379-9511; fax: (209) 379-9510; web: www.yni.org.

YOSEMITE NATIONAL PARK

STANISLAUS NATIONAL FOREST

Emigrant Wilderness

Styx Pass

Kibbie Lake

O'Shaughnessy Dam

h Hetchy Entrance

ather

Middle

ca

Big Oak Flat Entrance

Old Big Oak Flat Road
closed to vehicle traffic

TUOLUMNE GROVE

Crane Flat

MERCED GROVE

STANISLAUS NATIONAL FOREST

El Portal

rom Merced

from Merced

SIERRA NATIONAL FOREST

Haystack Peak

Schofield Peak

Richardson Peak
9877ft 3010m

Otter Lake

Twin Lakes

Mount Gibson

TILTILL VALLEY

Wapama Falls

Hetch Hetchy Reservoir

Hetch

Smith Peak
7751ft 2363m

Tuolumne River

Bald Mountain
7261ft 2213m

ASPEN VALLEY

White Wolf

Siesta Lake

Tioga Road

Tioga Road closed
November to May east of this point

Tamarack Creek

Cascade Creek

Three Brothers

El Capitan
7569ft 2307m

Tunnel

Tunnel

Tunnel

Inspiration Point

Bridalveil Fall

Old Inspiration Point

Glacier Point Road closed
November to May east of this point

Arch Rock Entrance

El Portal Road

SUMMIT MEADOW

Chinquapin

Yosemite West

HENNESS RIDGE

Badger Pass Ski Area

WESTFALL MEADOWS

Wawona Road

Alder Creek

TURNER RIDGE

Wawona

Pioneer Yosemite History Center

South Entrance

Mariposa Grove

Chilnualna Fall

Wawona Dome

South Fork Merced River

South Fork Merced River

Tower Peak

Buckeye Pass
9572ft 2917m

Twin Lakes

Tilden Lake

STUBBLEFIELD CANYON

JACK MAIN CANYON

Falls Creek

Pacific Crest Trail

KERRICK CANYON

Piute Mountain
10541ft 3213m

Piute Creek

PLEASANT VALLEY

Table Lake

RODGERS CANYON

Pettit Peak
10788ft 3288m

RANCHERIA MOUNTAIN

Rancheria Creek

Muir Gorge

THE TUOLUMNE RIVER

Waterwheel Falls

Tuolumne River

GRAND CANYON OF

Ten Lakes

May Lake

Tuolumne Peak
10845ft 3306m

Polly Dome

Yosemite Creek

Pothole Dome

120

TUOLUMNE MEADOWS

Fairview Dome

Medlicott Dome

Tuolumne Meadows Visitor Center

Cathedral Lakes

Cathedral Peak
10940ft 3335m

Elizabeth Lake

Unicorn Peak

Tenaya Lake

Olmsted Point

Snow Creek

TENAYA CANYON

Tenaya Creek

Yosemite Village

Valley Visitor Center

Yosemite Falls

North Dome

Clouds Rest

Moraine Dome

Half Dome
8842ft 2695m

Liberty Cap

Merced River

Merced Lake

LITTLE YOSEMITE VALLEY

Nevada Fall

John Muir Trail

Vernal Fall

Illilouette Fall

Washburn Lake

Merced Lake

YOSEMITE VALLEY

Cathedral Rocks

Sentinel Dome

Glacier Point

Glacier Point Road

HORIZON RIDGE

MONO MEADOW

Bridalveil Creek

Illilouette Creek

Ostrander Ski Hut

HORSE RIDGE

CLARK RANGE

Foerster Peak
12058ft 3675m

ANSEL ADAMS WILDERNESS

HOOVER WILDERNESS

Peeler Lake

Crown Lake

SAWTOOTH RIDGE

Slide Mountain

Matterhorn Peak

TOIYABE NATIONAL FOREST

MATTERHORN CANYON

VIRGINIA CANYON

Volunteer Peak

SPILLER CANYON

McCabe Creek

Virginia Lakes

Upper McCabe Lake

McCabe Lakes (Roosevelt Lake)

North Peak

Mount Conness

White Mountain

HALL NATURAL AREA

INYO NATIONAL FOREST

Lundy Lake

Saddlebag Lake

Tioga Peak
11526ft 3513m

From Lee Vining and
395

120

Ellery Lake

Tioga Lake

Granite Lakes

Tioga Pass Entrance

Tioga Road closed
November to May west of this point.

Delaney Creek

Pothole Dome

Lembert Dome

DANA MEADOWS

Mount Dana

Mount Gibbs

Ragged Peak

Pacific Crest Trail

LYELL CANYON

KUNA CREST

John Muir Trail

Amelia Earhart Peak

Donohue Pass

Pacific Crest Trail

Mount Lyell
13114ft 3997m

Lyell Fork

From Carson City, NV
395

TWIN LAKES

Twin Lakes

VICINITY MAP

Sacramento

NEVADA

108

49

120

99

Manteca

Modesto

5

YOSEMITE NATIONAL PARK

120

140

Lee Vining

Mono Lake

6
95

Yosemite Village

395

6

Bishop

Merced

41

Sequoia & Kings Canyon National Parks

180

Fresno

CALIFORNIA

N

From Fresno

Yosemite's Heritage

Already well over a century old, Yosemite National Park has demonstrated its worth to Americans and to people from all over the world. For generations it has been a vital part of our heritage. And as we are becoming more and more aware of the value—the need—for such islands of serenity in the modern world of ever-increasing industry, technology, and international political stress, the national-park concept is becoming more secure. Indeed, it seems utterly inconceivable that such a wonderful region as Yosemite National Park could ever be put to any other use.

Yosemite's treasures lie all around waiting to be noticed. Some are obvious, such as Half Dome and the way its cliff turns pink at sunset. But others, such as Yosemite's nighttime denizens, delicate wildflowers, and details such as the crystalline beauty of early-morning frost on grass, can easily go unnoticed in the shadow of Yosemite's spectacular features. These, and many, many more, are the treasures that lie in store for those who take the time to look and savor.

There is a story told in Yosemite that succinctly summarizes the appeal of the park and the infinite diversity of its wonders: A lady visitor, who wanted to spend her time in Yosemite to the best advantage, asked a park ranger, "What would you do if you had only one day to spend in Yosemite?" "Madam," the ranger replied, "I'd weep."

The "next generation," for whom Yosemite is established, enjoys his park.

TOM MYERS

KC Publications has been the leading publisher of colorful, interpretive books about National Park areas, public lands, Indian Culture, and related subjects for over 45 years. We have 5 active series – over 125 titles – with Translation Packages in up to 8 languages for over half the areas we cover.   Write, call, or visit our web site for our full-color catalog.

Our series are:

The Story Behind the Scenery® – Compelling stories of over 65 National Park areas and similar Public Land areas. Some with Translation Packages.

in pictures... Nature's Continuing Story® – A companion, pictorially oriented, series on America's National Parks.   All titles have Translation Packages.

For Young Adventurers® – Dedicated to young seekers and keepers of all things wild and sacred. Explore America's Heritage from A to Z.

Voyage of Discovery® – Exploration of the expansion of the western United States.

Indian Culture and the Southwest – All about Native Americans, past and present.

We publish over 125 titles – Books and other related specialty products.
   Our full-color catalog is available online or by contacting us:
Call (800) 626-9673, Fax (928) 684-5189, Write to the address below,
   Or visit our web site at www.nationalparksbooks.com
Published by KC Publications • P.O. Box 3615 • Wickenburg, AZ 85358

Inside Back Cover:
Cloud falls within the Valley create an aurora that becomes a lifetime happening. Photo by Jose F. Leis.

Back Cover: Townsley Lake in the Yosemite wilderness. Photo by Kathleen Norris Cook.

Created, Designed, and Published in the U.S.A.
Printed by Tien Wah Press (Pte.) Ltd, Singapore
Pre-Press by United Graphic Pte. Ltd